ALADDIN

AND

THE WONDERFUL

LAMP

A PICTURE BOOK

Walter Crane

[ZHINGOORA BOOKS]

ALADDIN,

AND THE WONDERFUL LAMP.

ALADDIN was the son of a poor tailor in an Eastern city. He was a spoiled boy, and loved play better than work; so that when Mustapha, his father, died, he was not able to earn his living; and his poor mother had to spin cotton all day long to procure food for their support. But she dearly loved her son, knowing that he had a good heart, and she believed that as he grew older he would do better, and become at last a worthy and prosperous man. One day, when Aladdin was walking outside the town, an old man came up to him, and looking very hard in his face, said he was his father's brother, and had long been away in a distant country, but that now he wished to help his nephew to get on. He then put a ring on the boy's finger, telling him that no harm could happen to him so long as he wore it. Now, this strange man was no uncle of Aladdin, nor was he related at all to him; but he was a wicked magician, who wanted to make use of the lad's services, as we shall see presently.

The old man led Aladdin a good way into the country, until they came to a very lonely spot between two lofty black mountains. Here he lighted a fire, and threw into it some gum, all the time repeating many strange words. The ground then opened just before them, and a stone trap-door appeared. After lifting this up, the Magician told Aladdin to go below, down some broken steps, and at the foot of these he would find three halls, in the last of which was a door leading to a garden full of beautiful trees; this he was to cross, and after mounting some more steps, he would come to a terrace, when he would see a niche, in which there was a lighted Lamp. He was then to take the Lamp, put out the light, empty the oil, and bring it away with him.

Aladdin found all the Magician had told him to be true; he passed quickly but cautiously through the three halls, so as not even to touch the walls with his clothes, as the Magician had directed. He took the Lamp from the niche, threw out the oil, and put it in his bosom. As he came back through the garden, his eyes were dazzled with the bright-coloured fruits on the trees, shining like glass. Many of these he plucked and put in his pockets, and then returned with the Lamp, and called upon his uncle to help him up the broken steps. "Give me the Lamp," said the old man, angrily. "Not till I get out safe," cried the boy. The Magician, in a passion, then slammed down the trap-door, and Aladdin was shut up fast enough. While crying bitterly, he by chance rubbed the ring, and a figure appeared before him, saying, "I am your slave, the Genius of the Ring; what do you desire?"

Aladdin told the Genius of the Ring that he only wanted to be set free, and to be taken back to his mother. In an instant he found himself at home, very hungry, and his poor mother was much pleased to see him again. He told her all that had happened; she then felt curious to look at the Lamp he had brought, and began rubbing it, to make it shine brighter. Both were quite amazed at seeing rise before them a strange figure; this proved to be the Genius of the Lamp, who asked for their commands. On hearing that food was what they most wanted, a black slave instantly entered with the choicest fare upon a dainty dish of silver, and with silver plates for them to eat from.

Aladdin and his mother feasted upon the rich fare brought to them, and sold the silver dish and plates, on the produce of which they lived happily for some weeks. Aladdin was now able to dress well, and in taking his usual walk, he one day chanced to see the Sultan's daughter coming with her attendants from the baths. He was so much struck with her beauty, that he fell in love with her at once, and told his mother that she must go to the Sultan, and ask him to give the Princess to be his wife. The poor woman said he must be crazy; but her son not only knew what a treasure he had got in the Magic Lamp, but he had also found how valuable were the shining fruits he had gathered, which he thought at the time to be only coloured glass. At first he sent a bowlful of these jewels—for so they were—to the Sultan, who was amazed at their richness, and said to Aladdin's mother: "Your son shall have his wish, if he can send me, in a week, forty bowls like this, carried by twenty white and twenty black slaves, handsomely dressed." He thought by this to keep what he had got, and to hear no more of Aladdin. But the Genius of the Lamp soon brought the bowls of jewels and the slaves, and Aladdin's mother went with them to the Sultan.

The Sultan was overjoyed at receiving these rich gifts, and at once agreed that the Princess Bulbul should be the wife of Aladdin. The happy youth then summoned the Genius of the Lamp to assist him; and shortly set out for the Palace. He was dressed in a handsome suit of clothes, and rode a beautiful horse; by his side marched a number of attendants, scattering handfuls of gold among the people. As soon as they were married, Aladdin ordered the Genius of the Lamp to build, in the course of a night, a most superb Palace, and there the young couple lived quite happily for some time.

One day, when Aladdin was out hunting with the Sultan, the wicked Magician, who had heard of his good luck, and wished to get hold of the Magic Lamp, cried out in the streets, "New lamps for old ones!" A silly maid in the Palace, hearing this, got leave of the Princess to change Aladdin's old Lamp, which she had seen on a cornice where he always left it, for a new one, and so the Magician got possession of it.

As soon as the Magician had safely got the Lamp, he caused the Genius to remove the Palace, and Bulbul within it, to Africa. Aladdin's grief was very great, and so was the rage of the Sultan at the loss of the Princess, and poor Aladdin's life was in some danger, for the Sultan threatened to kill him if he did not restore his daughter in three days. Aladdin first called upon the Genius of the Ring to help him, but all he could do was to take him to Africa. The Princess was rejoiced to see him again, but was very sorry to find that she had been the cause of all their trouble by parting with the wonderful Lamp. Aladdin, however, consoled her, and told her that he had thought of a plan for getting it back. He then left her, but soon returned with a powerful sleeping-draught, and advised her to receive the Magician with pretended kindness, and pour it into his wine at dinner that day, so as to make him fall sound asleep, when they could take the Lamp from him. Everything happened as they expected; the Magician drank the wine, and when Aladdin came in, he found that he had fallen back lifeless on the couch. Aladdin took the Lamp from his bosom, and called upon the Genius to transport the Palace, the Princess, and himself, back to their native city. The Sultan was as much astonished and pleased at their return, as he had been provoked at the loss of his daughter; and Aladdin, with his Bulbul, lived long afterwards to enjoy his good fortune.

End of the Book

www.ingramcontent.com/pod-product-compliance
Lightning Source LLC
Chambersburg PA
CBHW060022300526
45794CB00003B/1260